CAMEROON

...in Pictures

Courtesy of American Lutheran Church

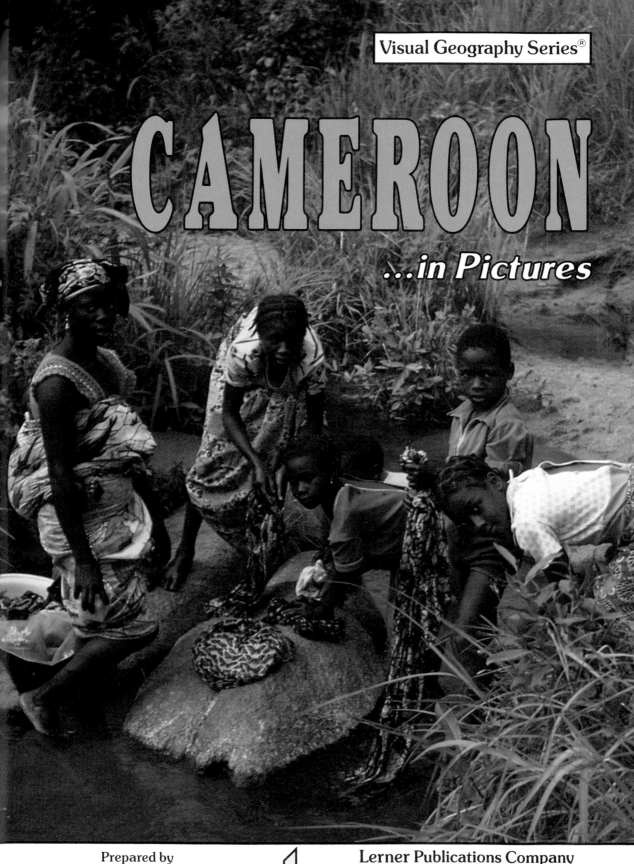

Visual Geography Series®

CAMEROON

...in Pictures

Prepared by
Jim Hathaway

Lerner Publications Company
Minneapolis

Courtesy of A. B. Hinderlie

**Young Cameroonians ride an empty cart on their way to
gather wood near their village.**

This is an all-new edition of the Visual Geography
Series. Previous editions have been published by
Sterling Publishing Company, New York City, and
some of the original textual information has been retained. New photographs, maps, charts, captions, and
updated information have been added. The text has
been entirely reset in 10/12 Century Textbook.

LIBRARY OF CONGRESS CATALOGING-IN-PUBLICATION DATA

Hathaway, Jim.
   Cameroon in pictures / prepared by Jim Hathaway.
    p. cm.—(Visual geography series)
   Includes index.
   Summary: An introduction to the geography, history,
economy, government, people, and culture of this cen-
tral African country situated on the Atlantic coast.
   ISBN 0-8225-1857-0 (lib. bdg.)
   1. Cameroon. [1. Cameroon.] I. Title.   II. Series:
Visual geography series (Minneapolis, Minn.)
DT564.H37 1989   88–31370
967'.11—dc19   CIP
                              AC

International Standard Book Number: 0-8225-1857-0
Library of Congress Card Catalog Number: 88-31370

VISUAL GEOGRAPHY SERIES®

Publisher
Harry Jonas Lerner
Associate Publisher
Nancy M. Campbell
Senior Editor
Mary M. Rodgers
Editors
Gretchen Bratvold
Dan Filbin
Photo Researcher
Karen A. Sirvaitis
Editorial/Photo Assistant
Marybeth Campbell
Consultants/Contributors
Jim Hathaway
Sandra K. Davis
Designer
Jim Simondet
Cartographer
Carol F. Barrett
Indexers
Kristine S. Schubert
Sylvia Timian
Production Manager
Richard J. Hannah

Photo by Bernice K. Condit

**A mother and child wait in line for a checkup at a clinic near
Ngaoundéré.**

Acknowledgements

Title page courtesy of Dr. Walter Blue.

Elevation contours adapted from *The Times Atlas of
the World*, seventh comprehensive edition (New York:
Times Books, 1985).

1 2 3 4 5 6 7 8 9 10 98 97 96 95 94 93 92 91 90 89

Courtesy of American Lutheran Church

Cameroonian triplets wake from their naps. At the 1988 population growth rate of 2.6 percent, Cameroon's population will double within 26 years.

Contents

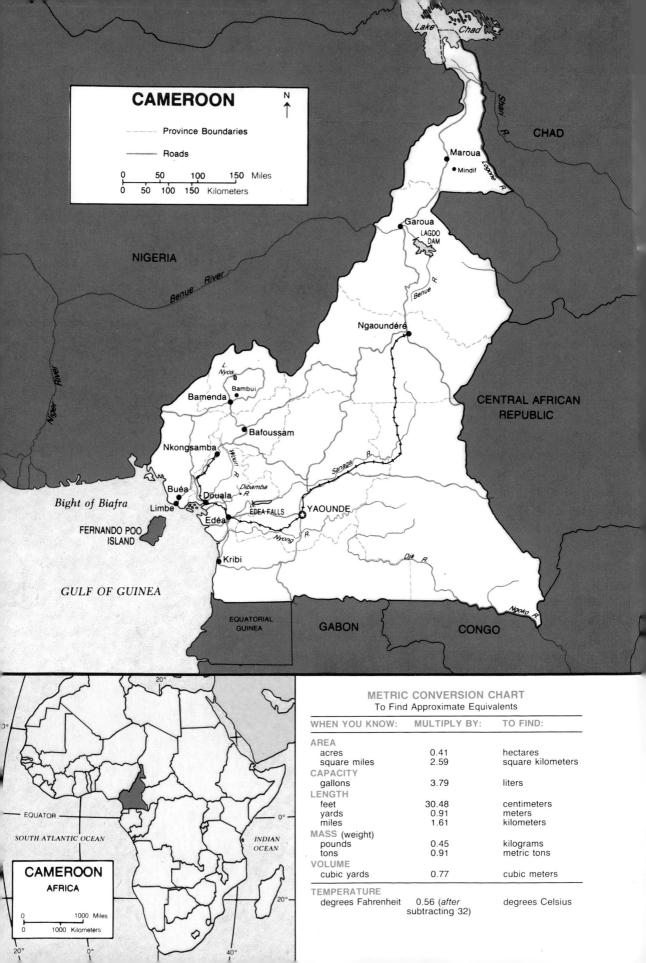

CAMEROON

N ↑

- - - - Province Boundaries
——— Roads

|0   50   100   150   Miles|
|0 50 100 150 Kilometers|

CHAD

Lake Chad

Shari R.

Logone R.

Maroua
• Mindif

Garoua
LAGDO DAM

Benue R.

NIGERIA

Benue River

Ngaoundéré

CENTRAL AFRICAN REPUBLIC

Niger River

L. Nyos
• Bambui
Bamenda

Bafoussam

Nkongsamba

Wouri R.

Sanaga R.

Buéa
Limbe
Douala
Dibamba R.
EDEA FALLS
Edéa
YAOUNDE

Nyong R.

Bight of Biafra

FERNANDO POO ISLAND

Kribi

Dja R.

GULF OF GUINEA

Ngoko R.

EQUATORIAL GUINEA

GABON

CONGO

20°

EQUATOR

0°

SOUTH ATLANTIC OCEAN

INDIAN OCEAN

CAMEROON
AFRICA

|0   1000   Miles|
|0 1000 Kilometers|

20°   0°   40°

20°

METRIC CONVERSION CHART
To Find Approximate Equivalents

WHEN YOU KNOW:	MULTIPLY BY:	TO FIND:
AREA		
acres	0.41	hectares
square miles	2.59	square kilometers
CAPACITY		
gallons	3.79	liters
LENGTH		
feet	30.48	centimeters
yards	0.91	meters
miles	1.61	kilometers
MASS (weight)		
pounds	0.45	kilograms
tons	0.91	metric tons
VOLUME		
cubic yards	0.77	cubic meters
TEMPERATURE		
degrees Fahrenheit	0.56 (*after* subtracting 32)	degrees Celsius

Courtesy of L. Everett

On the Adamawa Plateau in central Cameroon, dwellings often are made with mud-brick walls and thatched roofs. Most Cameroonians live in rural areas and follow a way of life not much different from that led by their ancestors 200 years ago.

Introduction

Located on the western coast of Africa, Cameroon's high mountains, ocean beaches, broad grasslands, and semi-arid scrublands are typical of the continent's varied landscapes. The diversity of Africa's people is also apparent in the more than 200 ethnic groups that live in Cameroon.

Some Cameroonians lead a centuries-old way of life in remote mountains or forests. Others live in large, modern cities, such as Yaoundé—the nation's capital—or Douala. The great majority of Cameroonians are farmers who are caught between deeply rooted traditions and the influences of modern ideas and technology.

The ancient peoples of what is now northern Cameroon traded goods across the Sahara Desert over 2,000 years ago. Ancestors of an ethnic group named the Douala, who inhabit Cameroon's coastal regions, were the first to have contact with Europeans. The Douala met Portuguese traders who had arrived on the coast of western Africa in the late fifteenth century. Beginning in the early sixteenth century, slave traders took large numbers of Cameroonians as captives. The slave raids continued in the region for the next three centuries.

Three different foreign nations used their power in Cameroon. In 1884 Germany became the first European country to form colonies in Cameroon. After World War I (1914–1918), the French took control

7

of the eastern part of the country, and the British occupied the western part. Modern Cameroon is one of the few African countries formed by merging territories with different colonial histories. It is also the only African nation that officially uses both the French and the English languages.

Under the leadership of Ahmadou Ahidjo, Cameroon achieved its independence in 1960. Ahidjo created a firmly controlled and highly centralized one-party govern-ment. Paul Biya, Cameroon's president since 1982, has continued this type of government but has also introduced some reforms. Together Ahidjo and Biya have overseen a long period of economic stability in Cameroon – something rarely seen in Africa.

Cameroon's economic outlook is more positive than that of many of its neighbors. With the help of diverse resources, of French assistance, of economic planning, and of the discovery of oil, Cameroon

In the late sixteenth century, European and African traders began taking people as slaves from the region of Cameroon. The slave trade continued for over 300 years.

Independent Picture Service

The sign posted at the entrance of this cooperative farm is written in English and French – the two official languages of Cameroon. Both languages are spoken throughout the country, although English predominates in the west and French is more common in the east.

Courtesy of L. Everett

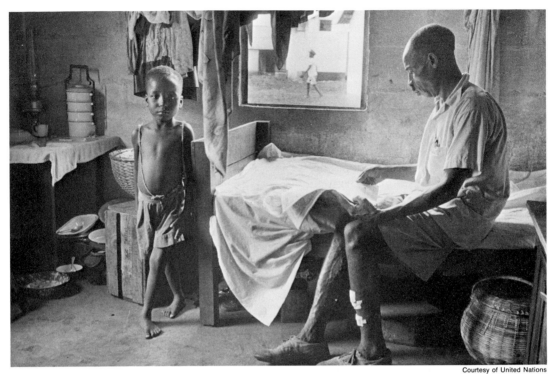

Some of Cameroon's people—especially in rural areas—have not received the economic benefits of the nation's recent oil boom.

has enjoyed long-term economic growth since the early 1970s.

The benefits of national development in Cameroon, however, have not been distributed evenly. People of the Christian south and west have a standard of living higher than that of inhabitants of the north who follow the Islamic religion. In addition, urban Cameroonians fare better than rural dwellers. Among other approaches, the government is trying to remedy the economic imbalance by renewing its emphasis on agricultural development. Through a series of five-year economic plans, Biya is taking what he calls *petit pas* (little steps) toward the overall improvement of Cameroon.

A young Cameroonian plays with the rim of a bicycle wheel. The nation has begun to place more of its resources in education and other services in the hope of developing its future labor force.

On their way to the town of Bamenda in southwestern Cameroon, villagers carefully carry wood down the slope of a rocky hillside. The landscape shows the effects of volcanic activity and of shifts in the earth's crust.

1) The Land

Lying just north of the equator along Africa's western coast, Cameroon is a roughly triangular piece of territory. The 700-mile-long western side of the country begins on the Gulf of Guinea—an inlet of the Atlantic Ocean. The western border then passes northward along the nation's boundary with Nigeria until the frontier reaches Lake Chad. Cameroon shares its eastern boundary with Chad in the north and with the Central African Republic in the east. Congo lies south and east of Cameroon. Gabon and Equatorial Guinea stretch along the southern base of Cam-

eroon. With an area of 183,569 square miles, Cameroon is a little larger than the state of California.

Topography

Cameroon has four topographical regions. In the southwestern corner lies a narrow coastal plain. A southern plateau combines with the Adamawa Plateau to form the country's second and largest topographical section, called central Cameroon. In the far north, a rolling plain—which turns into marshland as it approaches

Lake Chad—makes up the third region. The country's fourth region lies in the west and is composed of mountains and highlands.

COASTAL PLAIN

Flat marshland covers most of Cameroon's 160-mile-long coast on the Gulf of Guinea. Only towering Mount Cameroon (13,354 feet)—the highest peak in western Africa—intrudes along the coast. North-west of the peak, the plain is less than 20 miles wide. It then broadens in the south —extending 50 miles inland around the city of Douala—before narrowing again as the plain approaches the border with Equatorial Guinea. Cameroon's fast-flowing rivers deposit rich sediments on the coastal plain and empty into the Gulf of Guinea. The new soil creates fertile areas, called deltas, along the central part of the coast.

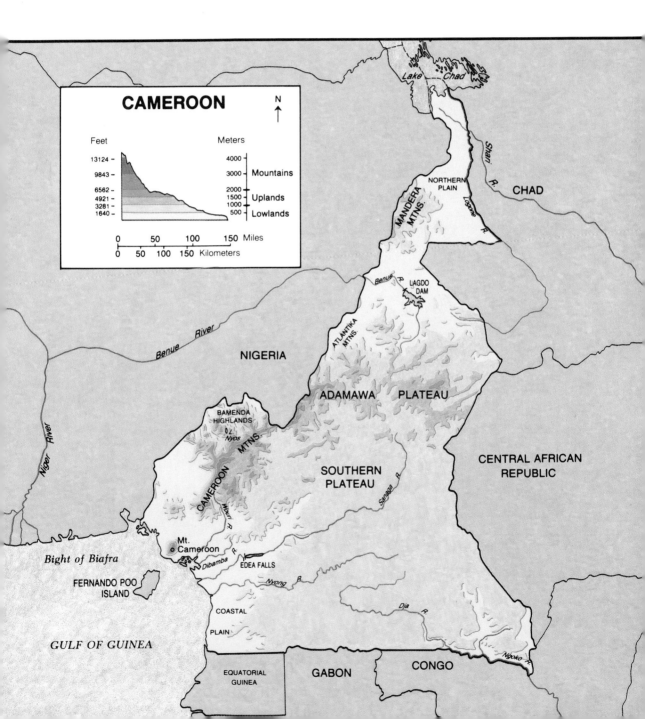

CENTRAL CAMEROON

Inland—and often marked by an abrupt change of altitude—the southern and Adamawa plateaus make up Cameroon's large central region. The southern plateau averages about 2,000 feet above sea level. Although the topsoil in this region is shallow and has a large percentage of granite, it supports thick forests.

The plateau gradually rises until it meets the Adamawa escarpment (cliff), which runs west to east in the middle of Cameroon. The Adamawa Plateau begins at this fracture line, which was formed by the shifting of the earth's crust millions of years ago. This second plateau reaches an average elevation of 3,500 feet.

Forests turn into savanna (grassland with scattered trees) in the northern section of the Adamawa Plateau. In the west, the plateau's soil consists of old volcanic lava that rests upon a granite base.

Courtesy of L. Everett

On the Adamawa Plateau, farmers sometimes build temporary shelters to live in while they harvest corn.

Courtesy of Dr. Walter Blue

Mindif, a small town on the northern plain, is scattered with grasses and trees that are typical of savanna vegetation.

High-yield corn crops are a common feature of the fertile lands of western Cameroon. At some elevations, however, chemical fertilizers are needed to promote corn growth in the region.

An isolated rock formation stands on a low plain in western Cameroon. Climatic conditions caused the rocky mass to erode into a distinctive shape.

THE NORTH

The Adamawa Plateau merges into the northern plain, which eventually enters the marshy basin that surrounds Lake Chad. Several rivers empty into the lake, including the Shari River. The Shari begins in the Central African Republic and forms the northernmost border of Chad and Cameroon. The fertile lands near the rivers support crops of cotton and peanuts.

WESTERN MOUNTAINS

Mountains, which extend along the length of Cameroon's western border, compose the fourth region of the country. At the southern end of this region, the Cameroon Mountains average 7,000 feet above sea level—the highest and largest range in the nation. Immediately to the north lie the Atlantika Mountains, and farther north rise the Mandara Mountains.

These ranges include a belt of volcanoes, most of which are inactive. Over the centuries, the lava and ash that have come from these volcanoes have enriched the

13

region's soil. Mount Cameroon—the only remaining active peak and Africa's largest volcano—last erupted in 1959, when streams of molten lava covered an area of several square miles.

Another portion of this volcanic region became active in 1986 at Lake Nyos in northwestern Cameroon. An underground explosion caused a cloud of poisonous gas to bubble up out of the lake. The gas killed 1,700 people, as well as thousands of cattle and other animals. Scientists in the late 1980s still could not explain the eruption.

Rivers

Cameroon's many rivers carry huge volumes of rainwater, which fall mainly in the southern and coastal areas of the country. The rivers travel across varied terrain, and

their many scenic waterfalls have great potential for producing hydroelectricity. The rough, often dangerous, course of the rivers also makes them almost impossible to use as transportation lanes. The Benue River in the north is the only waterway that is able to support the passage of cargo. The Benue flows west across Cameroon's dry northern lands and then moves into Nigeria. Even on this waterway, however, barges can operate for only two months of the year, when seasonal rainfall swells its banks.

Following a 550-mile course across the width of Cameroon, the Sanaga River is the longest in the country. It originates in the Adamawa Plateau, flows over the Edéa Falls, and creates a large delta as it enters the Gulf of Guinea. The Wouri, Dibamba, and Nyong also feed into deltas

With early morning fog in the background, the Sanaga River flows past a corn field. During the rainy season the water level rises several feet, completely submerging the sandbar in the middle of the waterway.

Courtesy of L. Everett

Seasonal rains have caused this small stream near Bamenda to overflow its banks. Rainfall is heaviest from April to October, with some areas receiving more than 100 inches of rain during this period.

The tropical wet zone—characterized by heavy rainfall in most areas and temperatures that average 85° F—covers the southern part of the country. Although the average rainfall in this zone is 100 inches per year, the seaward side of Mount Cameroon receives 360 inches of rain a year, making it one of the wettest places on earth.

In the middle section of the country, which has a tropical wet and dry climate, moist air from the Atlantic Ocean moves over Cameroon, bringing rain and humidity. The resulting wet season from April to October averages 55 inches of precipitation. During the rest of the year, hot air masses from the Sahara Desert dry out the area. Temperatures in this central zone are usually five degrees warmer than those in the southern region.

along the gulf. One other large river system, the Dja-Ngoko, travels southward out of Cameroon into the Zaire River.

Climate

Cameroon's mountainous topography and its location on the Gulf of Guinea affect the country's climate. Average temperatures are high and often exceed 90° F in the north. Rainfall is more plentiful on the coast than it is inland, with more rain in the southern half of the country. Damp, moist air above the Atlantic and hot, dry air over the Sahara Desert north of the country combine to form three broad climate zones in Cameroon. These zones are known as tropical wet, tropical wet and dry, and semi-arid.

Courtesy of A. B. Hinderlie

In November, when rainfall decreases, once-mighty rivers become slow streams. This riverbed in central Cameroon is nearly dry and will not become navigable again until May.

15

The thick branches of this baobab tree shade the weekly market of a village in central Cameroon. Baobabs lose their leaves during the dry season but store enough water in their trunks to survive.

In the semi-arid zone in the north, moisture-bearing Atlantic winds make brief appearances and leave only 25 inches of rain from May through September. For the remainder of the year, hot and very dry winds—known as harmattans—blow from the interior of Africa and leave traces of Saharan dust on almost every surface. This northern region has daytime temperatures of over 90° F. Nighttime temperatures often fall to 50° F.

Flora

Cameroon's diverse topography and many climates foster a great variety plant life. The vegetation in the country falls into three broad types—forest, savanna, and scrubland.

Tropical rain-forests, mangrove forests, and deciduous (leaf-shedding) forests are each represented in Cameroon. The tropical rain-forests in the southern part of the country get plenty of warmth from the sun and an abundance of moisture throughout most of the year. As a result, they contain many tree species—such as oil palms, bamboo, mahogany, teak, ebony, and rubber.

Mangrove forests consist of large evergreens that grow on the muddy banks of rivers and along Cameroon's rainy coast. In less rainy areas of the central interior, the vegetation has adapted to yearly dry periods. Most of the trees in this region shed their leaves for a month or two when there is little moisture in the soil.

Savannas dominate both the rolling plains in the north and the Adamawa Plateau. Thick woodland with a ground cover of grass characterizes the southern part of the plateau. Farther north the vegetation changes to open grassland with only scattered deciduous trees. During the dry winters, the grasses die off aboveground. Their root systems survive, however, and send up new shoots when the rains come.

Trees of the savannas often have thick bark and small, drought-resistant leaves. Farmers who use fire to clear land for agricultural and grazing purposes have reduced the number of trees on the savanna. Although grasses grow back quickly after being burned, many trees do not.

The scrubland in the extreme north is barren much of the year. Natural vegetation consists mostly of hardy grasses, thorny shrubs, and small trees. Near Lake Chad, the floodplains of the Logone and Shari rivers contain marsh grasses and other swamp plants.

Fauna

Cameroon is home to much wildlife. Herds of hooved animals, including buffalo, giraffes, and antelope, graze on the savannas. These creatures feed on the region's vegetation—such as herbs that grow at ground level and twigs that sprout on the highest treetops. Lions, panthers, and cheetahs prey on these grazing animals. Elephants, rhinoceroses, hippopotamuses, hyenas, baboons, and anteaters also live in the savanna. Birds of the savanna include ostriches, ducks, pigeons, and guinea fowl.

Some of these animals of the savanna also thrive in the southern forests. Other forest dwellers include gorillas, chimpanzees, and birds such as toucans and parrots. Flamingos, ibis, kingfishers, and storks inhabit the forest wetlands. Cameroon's mountainous areas form another habitat. Here, scientists have found unusual types of mice, which glide from tree to tree, as well as rare frogs, toads, and lizards.

Cameroon also has a large number of reptiles. Both poisonous and nonpoisonous

Courtesy of Vicki Morgan

Fallen trees have been lashed together to make a footbridge across a stream. Thick forests are typical of Cameroon's southern and coastal regions.

Courtesy of A. B. Hinderlie

African antelope roam a wide area as they graze on savanna vegetation. Both male and female antelope have horns, which grow from a bony core that extends from their skulls.

17

Baboons—which usually live in groups of about 40 members—find food among the roots, stems, and leaves of savanna plants. The animals are fierce fighters when facing enemies who threaten the group.

These hippopotamuses sun themselves on a sandy riverbank. They spend much of their time grazing on the vegetation in and near rivers, eating about 130 pounds of food each day.

snakes range in size from small, deadly vipers to large pythons. The tsetse fly—which carries parasites that cause sleeping sickness in humans and the deadly disease nagana in animals—is common in some of the lowland areas. Mosquitoes that transmit malaria are found throughout the country.

Many fish live in Cameroon's rivers and in the Gulf of Guinea. Shrimp thrive in coastal rivers and lagoons. Saltwater fish caught off the coast include mackerel, sardines, and sharks.

Cities

Cameroon has two major cities, and together they contain about half of the country's urban population. Douala, a port at the mouth of the Wouri River, is the commercial center of the nation and has 700,000 people. The inland city of Yaoundé serves as the political capital, with a population of 500,000.

Douala was named after the ethnic group that originally inhabited the port area and nearby villages. For several centuries, Europeans bought locally produced goods, as well as slaves, from the Douala people. The port now serves a vast region, including not only Cameroon but also landlocked nations, such as the Central African Republic and Chad. In 1985, 4.5 million tons of goods moved through the port, making it one of the busiest harbors in Africa.

Easy access to imported raw materials and to manufactured items has created a variety of industries in Douala. In addition, many of Cameroon's trading companies and banks have their headquarters in the city's tall, modern buildings. These economic activities in Douala have attracted a large number of newcomers—mostly the Bamiléké—who arrived from the western part of the country and who now form nearly half of the population of

Importers store the goods they receive in large warehouses in Douala. A port city, Douala also handles a large volume of trade for the Central African Republic—a landlocked nation located east of Cameroon.

A sculpture *(left)* at one of Yaoundé's main intersections combines traditional carvings with contemporary art forms. Yaoundé—the nation's capital—has experienced rapid population growth since independence in 1960.

the city. Many residents do their shopping in the city's large open-air markets. Made up of hundreds of small businesses, Douala's markets provide a great variety of domestic and imported goods.

German colonial leaders founded Yaoundé in 1888 as a military base between the Nyong and Sanaga rivers. A form of the African word *Ewondo,* Yaoundé was named after one of the ethnic groups that lives in the region. In 1921 the French, who were the next colonial power to occupy the area, chose the city as the administrative capital of their territory because of its pleasant climate. Yaoundé's elevation—more than 2,000 feet above sea level—and its inland location make it cooler and less humid than Douala.

Yaoundé grew slowly until the Cameroonians achieved independence in 1960.

Rural Cameroonians buy and sell goods at weekly markets held in small settlements throughout the country.

20

Since then, the city has expanded tenfold. Yaoundé's explosive population increase is partly due to the availability of governmental and commercial jobs. Yaoundé is located in the center of a rich agricultural area, and serves as a transportation hub —with many roads, railways, and airways. In addition, the capital houses the main campus of the University of Yaoundé.

Secondary Towns

For a long time, the settlement of Ngaoundéré survived only because of its cattle trade. This once-small town, however, has grown rapidly since the completion of two major transportation projects in the 1970s. The Trans-Cameroonian Railway, which travels the length of the country, goes to Ngaoundéré as its northern endpoint. The government also built a highway connecting Ngaoundéré to Kousseri in the far north.

Regional leaders helped develop Garoua, which lies on the Benue River, into a river port for northern Cameroon. The city's markets feature goods that come up the river by barge from Nigeria. Some of Garoua's port business, however, has been absorbed by the Trans-Cameroonian Railway at Ngaoundéré.

Several smaller towns scattered throughout the country serve as regional hubs. Nkongsamba, in the coffee-growing area of western Cameroon, is the destination of a railroad that the Germans built from Douala before World War I. Bafoussan, the major town of the Bamiléké, is a center for provincial administration in the western highlands. An administrative center situated at the base of Mount Cameroon, Buéa is the site of several German castles that remain from the period when it served as the capital of German Cameroons. Nearby, Limbe, a port on the Gulf of Guinea, exports produce from local plantations.

Workers unload a truckload of firewood for use in the city of Ngaoundéré. The wood—the main cooking and heating fuel for many Cameroonians—was gathered from the distant countryside.

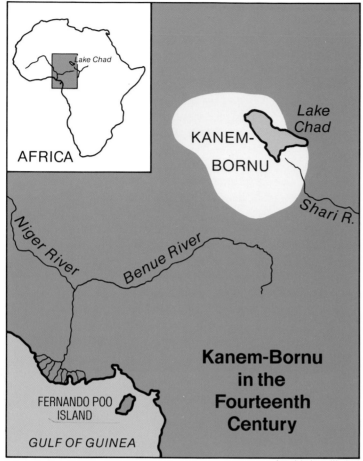

By the fourteenth century, the Kanem-Bornu Empire extended across portions of present-day Chad, Cameroon, and Nigeria. This empire was the first strong kingdom to emerge in this part of western Africa.

Artwork by Laura Westlund

2) History and Government

Evidence of early human settlement in Cameroon includes polished axes and spearheads, large stone monuments, and numerous cave drawings from the late Stone Age (about 8000 B.C.). Over the centuries, peoples from many parts of Africa moved through the territory that is now Cameroon, and some of them remained in the region. Ethnic groups that spoke Bantu languages arrived from eastern Africa. Other immigrants came from south of the Sahara Desert and from along the southern Atlantic coast.

Early History

The Sao, who lived near Lake Chad, organized the first known civilization in what is now Cameroon during the fifth century B.C. Twelve to fifteen hundred years later, Arab geographers and historians who traveled to the region referred to the Sao culture in their records. Many works of art, including bronze objects that date from the Sao period, have been uncovered.

Beginning in the late seventh century A.D., Arab peoples crossed the Sahara Desert in caravans to exchange goods with the Sao and with other groups living near Lake Chad. The Sao traded salt, leather, bronze, ostrich feathers, and ivory. Arab merchants often took Africans from these groups as slaves. The traders also converted some of the Africans in the region of the Sahel (the fertile land bordering the Sahara) to Islam. This one-god religion had been founded in Arabia by the prophet Muhammad in the mid-seventh century A.D.

Occasionally, large empires—which developed just south of the Sahara as early as the eighth century—extended their control into the northern part of present-day Cameroon. The dense forests of the region, however, blocked continued southward expansion by these empires.

The Kanem-Bornu Empire

The Kanem kingdom arose in the ninth century in the region east of Lake Chad. Ruled by *mais* (kings) who supervised trade across the Sahara Desert, the Kanem kingdom had become Islamic by the eleventh century. By the thirteenth century, the rulers of Kanem had extended their control over the Bornu region west of Lake Chad. In 1368, when attacks by eastern groups forced the Kanem court to flee its original home, the kingdom reestablished itself in the Bornu region.

The resulting Islamic Kanem-Bornu Empire was the first state to organize and

A guard for one of the leaders of a northern ethnic group wears ceremonial clothing that is very similar to styles of earlier centuries. Traditional Cameroonian leaders still have considerable power even though they have no official governmental authority.

control northern Cameroon. The new empire included a loose assembly of villages. At first the emperors of Kanem-Bornu rotated their headquarters from place to place, gathering taxes from each town. As time passed, however, the empire became more centralized.

New peoples migrated to southern Cameroon during Kanem-Bornu rule, but they did not push into the empire. The Douala arrived in the coastal region from present-day Congo and Zaire sometime before the fifteenth century. The Pahouin came from the Congo Basin and migrated first to the Adamawa Plateau before being pressured by other groups to move to the southern plateau. In the west, the Bantu-speaking Bamiléké had established themselves in the mountains by the sixteenth century. They extended their villages eastward until they met with resistance from the Bamoun group, which controlled the eastern part of the highland area.

After centuries of unbroken rule, the Kanem-Bornu realm eventually fell to the Fulbé, a nomadic, cattle-herding people who had entered the Lake Chad region from the western Sahara. In the nineteenth century, after the Fulbé had inhabited the area for several centuries, a devout Fulbé Muslim (follower of Islam) named Usman dan Fodio conquered the population of Kanem-Bornu.

Aided by skilled warriors and by superior military organization, Usman dan Fodio established a strict form of Islam from the Adamawa Plateau to present-day Nigeria. Mobido Adama, one of the Fulbé leaders, led an army that conquered the people living in Cameroon's central plateau, which now bears a variation of his name.

Portuguese Contact with Africa

Portuguese explorers were the first Europeans to approach Cameroon. The Portuguese established an outpost named São Tomé on an island in the Gulf of Guinea at the end of the fifteenth century. They

Courtesy of Eliot Elisofon, Eliot Elisofon Archives, National Museum of African Art, Smithsonian Institution

Fulbé soldiers were skilled at fighting from horseback. They swiftly conquered the declining Kanem-Bornu Empire during the nineteenth century.

fished on the mainland in the mouth of the Wouri River and caught crayfish that they believed to be prawns. The Portuguese called the river Rio dos Camarões (River of Prawns), from which the name Cameroon is derived. Explorers soon applied the name to the whole coastal area.

At first the Portuguese settled only on islands off the coast—perhaps because Europeans easily caught tropical diseases on the African continent. The Portuguese set up sugarcane plantations on the islands and traded with African merchants from the ethnic communities of the mainland. The Africans ferried their goods out to the Europeans, who conducted business either from their ships or from pontoons (flat-bottomed boats).

The Slave Trade

In addition to trading crops, the Portuguese and other foreigners engaged in the capture and exchange of human beings.

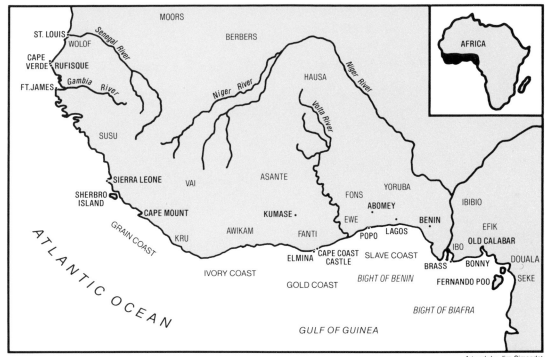

Europeans traded along the coast of western Africa. The territory that formed the Bight (bay) of Biafra—where Nigeria and Cameroon are located—was often used as a navigational landmark. The island of Fernando Póo lies just off the coast of Cameroon.

After enslaved Africans were ferried to oceangoing vessels, they endured a long journey under cramped living conditions. Many Africans died en route to the Americas.

Some African traders captured other Africans and sold them into slavery. Captives were forced to walk to the Gulf of Guinea, where members of the Douala acted as go-betweens for the slave-takers and the Europeans.

By the 1530s, the slave trade had spread rapidly along the coast of West Africa because plantation owners in the Americas sought a cheap labor force to harvest their crops. In response to this demand, Portuguese, Dutch, Spanish, British, French, and German slave traders exchanged salt, fabrics, and metals for captive humans from Africa.

British, French, and German merchants established semipermanent outposts on the mainland, especially along the Wouri River. The Douala served as brokers, providing a link between the Europeans and the African groups who captured other Africans from the interior to trade as slaves.

Britain outlawed slavery in its own territories in the early nineteenth century and tried to keep other nations from engaging in the trade. In 1827 the Spanish—who

After the slave trade declined in the nineteenth century, European traders sought alternative goods, such as palm oil and ivory. This decorative bowl was used to collect oil from the crushed fruit of oil palms.

Upon arriving in the Americas, African workers harvested sugarcane on large plantations. The sugar and molasses that the slaves produced were made into rum, which was then shipped back to Africa as a trade product. This three-part commercial arrangement was known as the "triangle trade."

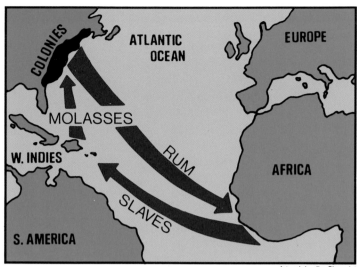

had taken control of São Tomé in the late eighteenth century—permitted the British to use the island as a base of operations for an antislavery campaign. The slave trade gradually diminished in Cameroon and the rest of Africa as the demand for new labor in the Americas declined. By the 1840s commerce in ivory and palm oil had become more profitable for European merchants than the slave trade.

The First Colonizers of Cameroon

During the nineteenth century, European powers—especially Britain, France, and Germany—began competing to colonize Cameroon. Great Britain had been slow to take advantage of opportunities to establish a protectorate along the coast of Cameroon in the 1870s. As a result, a German representative named Gustav Nachtigal negotiated territorial treaties with local

With a turban on his head, this ethnic leader dresses much the way his ancestors did. In the late 1800s, German and British colonizers rushed to make treaties with Cameroon's local ethnic leaders.

Douala leaders. In response, the British sent their own colonial officials to compete with the Germans for written treaties with other ethnic groups along the coast. The Germans, however, stayed one step ahead of the British and gained control of Cameroon in 1884.

As the German colonists moved inland, the Africans resisted them. After facing superior German firepower, many African groups signed agreements with the Germans. Under the terms of these documents, local authorities retained their positions but gave up ultimate control to a German administrator. On the other hand, some African groups successfully opposed the German advance for several years, and others never surrendered.

German colonial activities in Cameroon included trade and large-scale agriculture, both of which used forced labor. German colonists gained workers in two ways. Africans who had resisted German territorial advances were pressed into involuntary service through physical punishment. The

Photo by Bettmann Archive

Gustav Nachtigal, a representative of the German government, searched for Cameroonian leaders to persuade them to sign treaties in the 1880s. These agreements helped Germany dominate the territory of Cameroon.

Photo by Bettmann Archive

Many Cameroonians—particularly those who belonged to well-organized and well-armed ethnic groups—struggled against the advance of European colonization. German forces overcame most of the resisters but failed to gain control over the more able warriors, like these mounted soldiers from central Cameroon.

Christian missionaries from Europe and the United States built clinics, schools, and churches throughout Cameroon. Constructed by missionaries in the early twentieth century, this evangelical church is Douala's oldest religious building.

Germans also required local African leaders to assign workers to European planters and traders in order to fulfill a labor tax that was placed on each region. Some Cameroonian laborers were forced to collect palm oil, rubber, and ivory from the wilderness for use by German traders. Others cleared, planted, and tended land for plantation owners.

German farmers established many plantations in southwestern Cameroon and cultivated crops such as cacao (from which chocolate is derived), bananas, palm oil, and rubber. Large numbers of laborers were taken forcibly from their homes and sent to work in other parts of the country.

Unused to the different climates and sensitive to the diseases of new regions, these workers often became ill and died.

During their years of colonial rule, the Germans planned much of the region's transportation network. This development included wharves at Douala and other ports, rail lines from Douala north to Nkongsamba and east to Yaoundé, as well as many roads and bridges.

Christian missionaries from Germany, the United States, and Spain established several hundred schools in Cameroon at the end of the nineteenth and the beginning of the twentieth centuries. These schools were the primary centers of formal

29

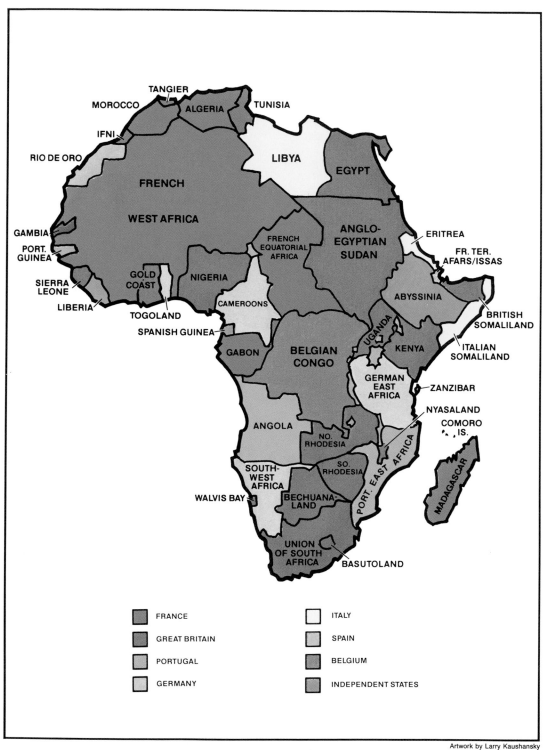

MOROCCO
TANGIER
ALGERIA
TUNISIA
IFNI
RIO DE ORO
LIBYA
EGYPT
FRENCH
WEST AFRICA
GAMBIA
PORT. GUINEA
FRENCH EQUATORIAL AFRICA
ANGLO-EGYPTIAN SUDAN
ERITREA
FR. TER. AFARS/ISSAS
SIERRA LEONE
GOLD COAST
NIGERIA
ABYSSINIA
LIBERIA
CAMEROONS
BRITISH SOMALILAND
TOGOLAND
SPANISH GUINEA
UGANDA
KENYA
ITALIAN SOMALILAND
GABON
BELGIAN CONGO
GERMAN EAST AFRICA
ZANZIBAR
NYASALAND
COMORO IS.
ANGOLA
NO. RHODESIA
SOUTH-WEST AFRICA
SO. RHODESIA
PORT. EAST AFRICA
MADAGASCAR
WALVIS BAY
BECHUANA-LAND
UNION OF SOUTH AFRICA
BASUTOLAND

FRANCE

GREAT BRITAIN

PORTUGAL

GERMANY

ITALY

SPAIN

BELGIUM

INDEPENDENT STATES

Artwork by Larry Kaushansky

By the late nineteenth century, European powers had carved the continent of Africa into areas of influence. Germany controlled Cameroon until the early twentieth century when France and Great Britain took over. (Map information taken from *The Anchor Atlas of World History*, 1978.)

30

French officers with troops from Senegal, a colony in French West Africa, march along a Yaoundé road during World War I (1914–1918). The allied French and British forces defeated the Germans in Cameroon in 1916.

education during the colonial era. Missionaries also built medical clinics to help control diseases such as leprosy, malaria, and smallpox.

World War I and Its Aftermath

During World War I (1914–1918), French and British troops—who were allied against Germany in the global conflict—invaded Cameroon in 1914. The French attacked from Gabon, their territory south of Cameroon, and the British assaulted the country from Nigeria in the west. After two years of fighting, the British and the French drove out the German forces.

The French took possession of about 80 percent of the country, and the British occupied two separate areas along the Nigerian border. In 1922 France and Britain agreed to administer their sections of Cameroon under the guidance of an international alliance called the League of Nations. The larger French territory became known as Cameroun, and the two smaller pieces of territory were named British Cameroons. The League of Nations set guidelines to help eliminate abuses of colonial power.

The League of Nations collapsed after World War II (1939–1945) and was replaced by the United Nations (UN). The new organization used guidelines that were similar to those set up by the league. The Cameroonian territories became trusteeships of the UN. This arrangement allowed the international body to supervise the British and French administration of the area.

BRITISH CAMEROONS

The British largely ignored their Cameroonian territory because it seemed remote and of little value to them. The region was divided into northern and southern portions, which were administered as part of Nigeria (a British colony from 1907 to 1960). Many Nigerians moved into British Cameroons to gain positions of economic importance—a development that Cameroonians regarded as an intrusion.

British Cameroons contained former German plantations that had been taken over by the British during World War I. Because there were few British buyers interested in the plantations, about 75 percent of the croplands were repurchased by Germans (who would again be expelled during

World War II). After the second global war began in 1939, a new governmental agency—the Cameroon Development Corporation—administered the plantations.

FRENCH CAMEROUN

The French took a much more active role in governing Cameroun than the British did in running their portion of the territory. France made substantial public and private investments in the country, with much of the effort concentrated around Douala and Yaoundé. The French supervised the construction of roads, the enlargement of Douala's port, and the development of more plantations. The territory's economy grew rapidly as large-scale farmers cultivated crops—such as coffee and cotton—for foreign sale rather than for local consumption.

The French achieved this growth in part by continuing the labor tax that was first employed by German colonists. The French also physically abused their laborers. Africans resented the harsh French policies, and both the League of Nations and the UN worked to put an end to forced labor.

Many Africans also resented the French colonial legal system. It separated "assimilated" Cameroonians—those Africans who had been educated by the French and lived a Western lifestyle—from "natives,"

German colonists established plantations in the early twentieth century that were still productive in the late twentieth century. This Cameroonian in the Bamenda Highlands is spraying coffee plants—one of the crops brought to the region by German landowners—with pesticides.

People of the Bamiléké ethnic group celebrate the selection of a new leader. Many members of Cameroonian ethnic groups still honored traditional channels of authority during colonial times. Their refusal to adopt Western ways made them unpopular among the French, who discriminated against those who held to their African heritage.

who maintained their African way of life. The French laws inflicted heavy penalties for minor offenses committed by non-Westernized Africans.

Steps Toward Independence

The charter that established the UN in 1945 promised eventual independence to all UN trust territories. This goal—combined with the growing discontent of many Africans—led to the growth of Cameroonian nationalist movements.

One of these movements was made up mainly of members of the Bamiléké ethnic group. In French Cameroun, this organization developed into the militant Union of Cameroonian Peoples (known by its French abbreviation, UPC). The first party to demand independence from colonial rule, the UPC also sought to combine the French and British territories into one nation.

After several years of political activity—which failed to bring either independence or unification—the UPC organized a revolt. Fighting erupted in May 1955, and several hundred city dwellers died in street riots. The rebellion received little support, however, because many Cameroonians

33

In the 1950s the UPC—the first group to organize in favor of a self-governing state—pictured a crab on their flag. UPC guerrilla fighters used the flag as a unifying symbol of their independence movement.

Artwork by Laura Westlund

believed an armed revolt would not gain independence. As a result, the uprising quickly lost momentum.

The government outlawed the UPC, and its members went into exile. Ruben Um Nyobé, one of the group's leaders, returned in 1957 to lead a guerrilla revolt that continued unevenly until 1962. During the prolonged conflict, approximately 20,000 Cameroonians died.

The activity of the UPC sparked other Cameroonians to pursue self-rule. André-Marie Mbida and Ahmadou Ahidjo were leaders of political parties that sought independence for French Cameroun.

In 1957 France permitted its overseas territories, including French Cameroun, to elect legislative assemblies. Mbida, the first prime minister of the Cameroonian assembly, proved to be an ineffective leader who lasted only a short time. Ahidjo, the leader of the Union Camerounaise (UC) party and Mbida's vice premier, assumed power in 1958. A Muslim from the north and a former schoolteacher, Ahidjo wanted to continue close ties with France. The Ahidjo government, with French support, limited the activity of the UPC rebels in Cameroon.

Independence and Unification

Cameroonians and the UN continued to pressure the French to grant the African colony self-rule. In 1958 the UN ended the French trusteeship over the region, and France gave Cameroonians internal control in 1959. The Republic of Cameroon declared its independence from France on January 1, 1960, and Ahidjo took office as the country's first president.

INDEPENDENCE OF BRITISH CAMEROONS

Until the mid-1950s Cameroonians in the British territories put their political energy into Nigerian politics. In 1955 John Foncha organized the Kamerun National Democratic party (KNDP), which called for British Cameroons to break off relations with Nigeria and for the territories to unite with French Cameroun. That same year, Emmanuel Endeley formed the Kamerun National Convention (KNC), which proposed the opposite course—

complete unification with Nigeria. In 1957 Endeley and the KNC won the majority of seats in the British Cameroons House of Assembly, but two years later Foncha and the KNDP won the majority.

In 1961 Foncha and Endeley supported a UN-supervised vote to decide the future of British Cameroons. The people in the northern section elected to become a province within newly independent Nigeria. Voters in the southern region, already resentful of Nigerian economic dominance, chose to unite with the Republic of Cameroon. The southern British territory joined Cameroon on October 1, 1961, forming the new Federal Republic of Cameroon, and John Foncha became vice president of the united nation.

UNIFICATION

Cameroon became a federation with a French-speaking eastern state and an English-speaking western one. Each had its own government, but they shared some federal services, such as education, transportation, and economic planning.

Running two separate governments, however, was expensive, and pressures grew to set up a central administration. In 1966 the political parties of both regions merged into the single Cameroonian National Union (known by its French initials, UNC). The UNC became the official state party and the only one allowed to sponsor candidates running for elected office.

A nationwide public vote held in 1972 changed Cameroon from a federation of two states into a centralized state. This newly reorganized country was called the United Republic of Cameroon.

Ahidjo's Presidency

Ahmadou Ahidjo became the dominant figure in independent, unified Cameroon. Elected president five times between 1960 and 1980, Ahidjo maintained political and economic stability in Cameroon for 22

Courtesy of Professor Victor T. LeVine

In 1961 people in British Cameroons lined up to vote in a UN-supervised election that was held to determine the future of their territory. The voters of the northern region opted to join Nigeria, and those in the southern part of the British colony chose to become part of Cameroon.

In 1980 President Ahmadou Ahidjo attended a conference of African nations in Sierra Leone, a nation in West Africa. Ahidjo brought a measure of order and prosperity to Cameroon at the price of limiting free expression in the political arena.

years. The price of stability, however, was government censorship of newspapers and curtailment of free speech. Many of Ahidjo's critics were English-speaking Cameroonians, who were outnumbered by the large French-speaking population. Because of their minority status, English-speaking Cameroonians felt disadvantaged within the united state.

Ahidjo also maintained control through his shrewd political appointments. For example, rather than favoring northerners from his home region, he appointed people from many areas of the country and from many different ethnic groups to serve as government officials. At times, he even gave political opponents prestigious jobs. Unfortunately, this system of political job placement also helped create a large, inefficient, and often corrupt bureaucracy.

Ahidjo proved to be a skilled manager of the nation's foreign relations. He main-

tained strong ties with France, which remained Cameroon's primary source of foreign aid. At the same time, Ahidjo did not align Cameroon too closely with any group of nations and thus received funds from both Eastern- and Western-bloc countries.

Biya and the 1980s

In November 1982, Ahidjo suddenly resigned in the middle of his fifth presidential term. He chose as his successor Prime Minister Paul Biya. A Christian southerner, Biya completed Ahidjo's term of office. Biya was elected to a full term as president in January 1984. One of his first acts was to change the country's name from the United Republic of Cameroon to the Republic of Cameroon.

Most Cameroonians expected Biya to follow Ahidjo's policies and to keep the

Ethnic and military representatives of both Christian and Muslim backgrounds review a parade during a civic celebration in Garoua. Cameroonian government officials, especially in northern Cameroon, work closely with traditional leaders.

Courtesy of Vicki Morgan

former president's cabinet ministers. But Biya installed several new cabinet members and made independent decisions. Cameroonian contacts with other nations, for example, became more productive under Biya's leadership. Politicians and business leaders, who had grown wealthy under Ahidjo, felt threatened by reforms that Biya proposed. In addition, some northerners resented Biya because he was a southerner.

In April 1984, members of the presidential guard—which was supposed to protect the president—attempted to overthrow the government. Most of the guard's members were from the north. The revolt took Biya and the army by surprise, and fighting broke out in Yaoundé. Although government troops crushed the rebellion within a few days, about 70 people were killed. The leaders of the attempted revolt were quickly tried and executed.

Photo by Peter Souza/The White House

President Paul Biya of Cameroon spoke with U.S. president Ronald Reagan during a visit to Washington, D.C. in 1986. A U.S. loan of over $25 million in 1985 helped Biya to enact development programs in Cameroon. Biya's reforms in the late 1980s gave Cameroonians a wider choice in electing national representatives.

After this outbreak of unrest, Biya increased his control through a series of government reorganizations. The president restructured government departments, dismissed his opponents or gave them less influential positions, and brought officials who were loyal to him into the government. In the late 1980s, the president received more popular support because he introduced a new policy that permitted several candidates to run for office in Cameroon's one-party state. As a result, voters may choose from many possibilities in political elections, instead of having only one, party-approved candidate on the ballot for each post.

Government

Cameroon's constitution—adopted in 1972 and revised in 1975—provides for a president with strong authority. Elected by the voters to a five-year term, the president appoints a cabinet, proposes legislation, leads the military, makes treaties, and has broad emergency powers. The president and all major office holders in the nation must be nominated by the national political party—the UNC. In 1985 this group was renamed the Democratic Assembly of the Cameroonian People. All citizens over 21 years of age are allowed to vote.

The legislature is a one-house national assembly of 150 members, who are elected every five years. The assembly meets twice a year and passes legislation by a majority vote. Both the president and assembly members may initiate bills for consideration.

At the top of Cameroon's judicial system is a supreme court, which receives cases from appeals courts and other lower courts. Ethnic groups throughout the country also have traditional laws and judges. The government accepts these local judicial proceedings, except when they contradict national law.

Cameroon has 10 provinces, each of which is headed by a presidentially appointed governor with the help of an administrative staff. The provincial governments are represented in the president's cabinet by the minister of territorial administration.

Artwork by Laura Westlund

In Cameroon's three-color flag, green represents the forests of the southern region, and yellow signifies the savanna of the northern part of the country. The central yellow star on the red section of the flag symbolizes the unity of all Cameroonian regions.

Many people in Cameroon transport goods from place to place by carrying the loads on their heads. This method leaves the hands free and safely distributes the weight of the burden.

3) The People

In 1988, 10.5 million people lived in Cameroon. As in many African countries, Cameroon's population is growing at a very fast rate—2.6 percent per year. If the present birth rate continues, the number of Cameroonians will double in 26 years.

About 58 percent of Cameroon's people reside in rural regions. Urban areas are growing quickly, however, as are the side effects of rapid growth—unemployment and crime. The population of the country is distributed unevenly, with the western coast, southern plateau, and northern savanna having the highest concentrations of people. The eastern region and the Adamawa Plateau, in comparison, are sparsely settled.

Ethnic Groups

Cameroon has an unusually diverse mixture of peoples, with more than 200 ethnic communities. No one group dominates the entire country, and tensions exist between some of the clans. Because there are so many groups, some of them have been clustered into broad categories by social scientists. The two largest of these clusters are the Western Highlanders, who account for more than one-fifth of the nation's population, and the Pahouin, who make up a little less than one-fifth. Other sizable groups are the Douala, Bassa-Bakoko, Aka, and Fulbé.

THE WESTERN HIGHLANDERS

The Western Highlanders include the closely related Bamiléké, Tikar, and Bamoun peoples who live in the western mountain region. The Bamiléké are the largest of these groups. For decades, farmland has been in short supply among the Bamiléké, and many of them have moved to cities. Urban Bamiléké have developed business skills and hold merchant and professional positions in Yaoundé and Douala. Their success in commercial and professional life has sometimes led to conflict with more traditional groups.

The Tikar are farmers who are sometimes called "grassfielders" because of the grassy vegetation in the Bamenda Highlands where they live. Like the Bamiléké and Tikar peoples, the neighboring Bamoun also farm. Sultan Njoya was a Bamoun leader of the early twentieth century. A man of many achievements, he invented the first alphabet for the Bamoun language and recorded the history of his people.

THE PAHOUIN

The Pahouin group is made up of the Eton, Ewondo, Boulou, Fang, and other widely scattered groups. These peoples inhabit the forested area south of Yaoundé and speak Bantu-based languages. The Pahouin are mostly farmers. Christian missionaries strongly influenced the Pahouin and converted many of them to Christianity during the first half of the twentieth century.

THE BASSA-BAKOKO AND THE DOUALA

The Bassa-Bakoko and the Douala peoples live along riverways and along the Gulf of Guinea. Many of them fish and

Besides Cameroon's main ethnic groups, the nation includes dozens of smaller communities of peoples. Among these groups are the Bana, whose members gathered in 1982 to honor their new leader, or chief.

The palace of the traditional leaders of the Douala people was built in the nineteenth century in the city of Douala. Most Douala live in coastal regions of Cameroon, and many make their living by fishing in rivers and streams.

grow crops, such as cacao and bananas, for a living. Others are merchants. The numerous and predominantly Christian Bassa-Bakoko live in the southern part of the Sanaga River Valley. A history of forced labor and other disruptions by Europeans prompted the Bassa-Bakoko to join the UPC rebellion of the 1950s.

The first people to have contact with the Europeans in the late fifteenth century, the Douala were also the first to trade with foreigners and to be educated in the European tradition. Because many other Cameroonians have immigrated to the city of Douala in the twentieth century, the Douala are now a minority in their home territory.

THE AKA AND THE FULBÉ
The Aka, who are few in number, were probably the first residents of Cameroon's rain-forests. Of small physical stature—

This small Fulbé village lies in Cameroon's northwest province and contains both traditional and modern dwellings. The thatched, pointed roofs and circular clay walls contrast with the square, tin-roofed structures of concrete.

Within Cameroon, 200 African languages, plus English and French, are spoken. Although 67 percent of Cameroon's school-age children attend classes, few go on to secondary institutions.

many of them stand between four and five feet in height—the Aka are well adapted to the rain-forest environment. They remain food gatherers and bow-and-arrow hunters who trade meat and skins for salt, spear points, and cloth with their settled neighbors.

The Fulbé are the dominant group in northern Cameroon. These once-nomadic shepherds and skilled warriors now live in permanent villages, where they raise cattle and farm the land. Traditional Fulbé chiefs are well-respected and exert much influence in the northern towns of Maroua, Garoua, and Ngaoundéré.

Language

The languages introduced to the region by the colonial powers have created a gulf between French-speaking eastern Cameroon and English-speaking western Cameroon. At the time of unification, the government made both languages official to increase national unity. Radio and television stations broadcast in French and English, as well as in some of the African languages of the region. The leading government-owned newspaper is published daily in French, and its companion weekly appears in English. All official documents and forms are printed in both languages.

Two hundred African languages are spoken in Cameroon. Some of the major tongues include Fulfulde—the Fulbé language—and Ewondo, which is spoken by the southern Pahouin. Wes Cos, used in the western region, is a type of Pidgin English. It developed through African contact with English-speaking traders and missionaries and is a mixture of English and African languages.

Education

The Cameroonian government provides free education in public schools and offers

These science pupils are among 17,000 students enrolled at the University of Yaoundé, the main center of higher education in Cameroon.

financial aid to those students who attend private institutions. Class attendance is required of students in grades one through six, and all schools offer a bilingual (two-language) program of studies.

About 67 percent of Cameroon's school-age population goes to school, giving the nation one of the highest enrollment rates in Africa. Nearly all southern children of primary school age are enrolled, but fewer than 20 percent of potential students attend classes in some northern areas.

Male and female enrollment rates are also very different. Seventy-five percent of school-age boys attend classes, while only 59 percent of girls do. Few students continue studies in secondary institutions. In the mid-1980s, enrollment surveys recorded over 1.6 million students in elementary schools. Only 238,000 pupils attended secondary institutions.

The University of Yaoundé, founded at Yaoundé in 1962 with assistance from the French government, is the country's main university. Branch campuses are located in Douala, Buéa, and Ngaoundéré. University enrollment was 17,113 in the mid-1980s. Technical schools during the same period had 77,555 students.

Health

As in many other developing countries, Cameroon's high health risks are related

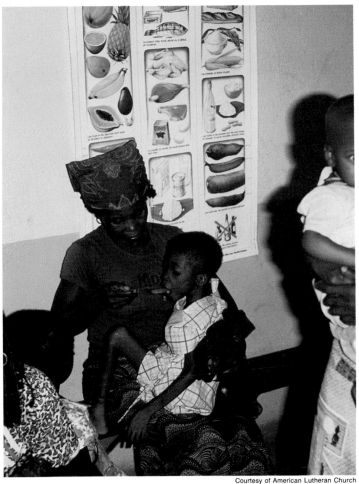

Beneath a poster that describes nutritionally rich foods, a woman feeds an ailing child at a local medical clinic.

Courtesy of American Lutheran Church

43

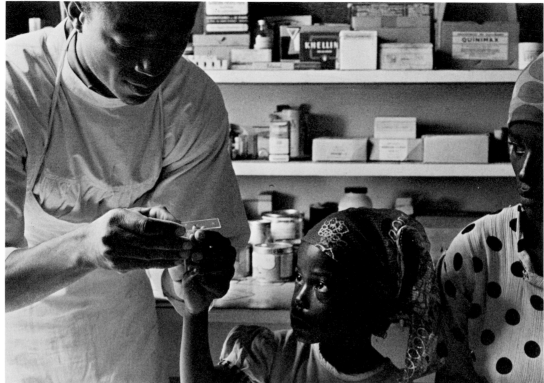

Most health services are concentrated in urban areas. Here, a medical assistant tests a young patient for malaria – a common ailment in Cameroon.

to unsafe drinking water, inadequate sanitation, nutritionally poor diets, and the lack of basic medical care. The most prevalent disease in the nation is malaria. Widely available medicines reduce the aches and fevers of this illness but do not prevent it. Sleeping sickness and river blindness, spread by insects that carry parasites, remain health threats despite many attempts to eliminate them. Other significant diseases are schistosomiasis (a disease that affects some internal organs), typhoid fever, yellow fever, and cholera.

A child clothed in a discarded plastic sheet drinks from a gourd. Water – especially in Cameroon's rural areas – is often unsafe for drinking and causes many diseases.

Medical professionals have made progress in improving the health of many Cameroonians. Life expectancy has increased from 45 years in 1965 to 50 years in 1988. Over the same period, the number of infants who died out of every 1,000 live births declined from 143 to 126. Cameroon's health statistics are somewhat less favorable than are the figures for Africa as a whole, where life expectancy is 52 years and the infant mortality rate is 110 per 1,000 live births.

Residents of rural areas live under difficult health conditions. In 1987, for example, only 26 percent of the population in the countryside had access to safe water. People living outside the cities are more likely to reject modern health care in favor of traditional practices, which often are ineffective.

The Arts and Recreation

Music and dance are a central part of many religious and social functions in Cameroon. Births, rites of passage into adulthood, weddings, and funerals have their own special dances and music. Musicians often use percussion instruments such as drums, xylophones, rattles, and scrapers to create sounds that blend African, European, and U.S. influences. Cameroon's most popular modern musician is saxophonist Manu Dibango, who plays a form of music called African jazz.

In Cameroon, as in most of Africa, traditional art is often functional rather than simply decorative. Sculpture almost always has religious meaning. Dancers wear finely carved masks during special occasions. Cameroonians house the masks in shrines when these artworks are not in use.

Courtesy of American Lutheran Church

Some of Cameroon's health problems are due to inadequate nutrition. Cassavas—a root crop that forms much of the Cameroonian diet but has little nutritional value—can be prepared several ways. This woman is making a kind of bread from crushed cassava.

Courtesy of American Lutheran Church

Sharply carved masks reveal the artistic talent of Cameroonian craftspeople as well as the influence of the nation's traditional culture on modern art forms.

A mounted Islamic warrior with a raised spear is the subject of this Cameroonian sculpture and may represent the conquest of northern Cameroon by Fulbé soldiers in the nineteenth century.

Oral literature is highly developed in Cameroon and has many uses. Some spoken literature brings Cameroonians into contact with the world of their ancestral spirits. Other oral traditions include riddles, satires, proverbs, poems, and fables that storytellers recite to entertain and instruct their listeners.

Two of Cameroon's best-known modern writers are Mongo Beti and Ferdinand Oyono, who both write in the French language. Beti's novels explore the conflict between African and Western values. One of his novels, for example, emphasizes the destructive impact that Christian missions

have had on the traditional life of Cameroon's ethnic groups. Oyono highlights the negative side of colonialism in his work. A diplomat as well as a novelist, Oyono has held posts in the UN.

Soccer is Cameroon's national sport and ranks ahead of films, concerts, and other spectator activities as the most popular form of entertainment. Cameroonian pride swelled when the country's national soccer team won several games in the 1982 World Cup competition.

First held in 1973, an annual 19-mile footrace to the top of Mount Cameroon and back is one of the nation's unique

Dressed in ceremonial clothing, these Cameroonian men celebrate the coronation of their local leader by performing ancient dances.

sporting events. Starting in the town of Buéa (elevation 3,000 feet), competitors run through rain-forest, open savanna, and scrubland, as well as on hardened volcanic lava. The temperature at the beginning of the race is often above 70° F but falls to 32° F at the summit of the mountain.

Religion

Christianity, Islam, and traditional African religions are protected under the law in Cameroon. Both Christian and Muslim Cameroonians often also hold ancient African beliefs. For example, some Cameroonian Christian sects permit the custom of polygyny, which allows a husband to have

Young Cameroonians frequently practice soccer—the country's national sport.

several wives. Officially, 40 percent of Cameroon's population follow traditional religious beliefs, 40 percent practice Christianity, and 20 percent support the Islamic faith.

Followers of native African religions believe in a creator-god with whom they communicate through prayer and through ceremonial rites. According to this belief system, a living force unites the spiritual and material worlds. Africans who follow the religion of their ancestors also revere the spirits of the dead and regard the living and the dead as one community.

Islam is based on the teachings of Muhammad, a prophet from the Arabian Peninsula. Traveling in trade caravans across the Sahara Desert as early as the eleventh century, Arabs converted many northern Cameroonians to Islam. This religion requires its followers—called Muslims—to adhere to certain practices. These include praying five times a day, fasting, giving to the poor, and making a pilgrimage to Muhammad's birthplace in Saudi Arabia.

Christian missionaries arrived in Cameroon in the late nineteenth century and

Courtesy of Dr. Walter Blue

One-fifth of the people in Cameroon are Muslims (followers of the Islamic religion) and attend mosques (houses of prayer), such as this one in Ngaoundéré. Most Muslims combine Islamic ideas with traditional African beliefs.

Courtesy of American Lutheran Church

This Muslim ethnic leader wears a turban whose style is hundreds of years old. Within traditional Cameroonian society, the leader has authority over both religious and political matters.

Photo by Bernice K. Condit

Courtesy of American Lutheran Church

Storing gourds of food on a roof allows the items to ripen out of the range of many insects and other small, ground-dwelling animals.

began to convert people to Christianity. Roman Catholicism, the largest Christian denomination in Cameroon, is most widespread in the French-speaking eastern areas. Protestantism dominates in the western region. Christian missions continue to play an important role in education and health care in Cameroon.

Food

The Cameroonian diet consists mostly of foods such as roots, tubers (underground stems), millet (grain), fish, and milk from dairy animals. These items are generally found locally within each region. Corn, cassavas (starchy roots), tomatoes, and sweet potatoes were introduced from other areas of the world.

49

Transporting and storing food is difficult in many parts of the country. As a result, Cameroonians eat staple foods that are available from local producers. By and large, the national diet contains plenty of carbohydrates and starches but not enough protein. Throughout the country, people often enjoy their food in the form of thick soups with hot, spicy seasonings.

In the north, millet and sorghum serve as staple foods, and fermented beverages are prepared from them. Cattle and goats graze in the region near Lake Chad. The Fulbé rarely eat meat. Milk—fresh, curdled, or whipped into butter—is their main source of protein. The southern forest peoples rely on roots and tubers, especially yams and cassavas, for much of their food supply. Cameroonians often make cassavas into a flour called *gari*, which can be stored for up to several years.

A great variety of tropical fruits and vegetables—including bananas, pineapples, oranges, grapefruit, mangoes, and peppers—grow in southern and coastal Cameroon at different times of the year. Monkeys and some kinds of rodents are sources of meat, but they have become less available as settlements have expanded, causing the number of animals to decline. Beef, chicken, and pork are expensive throughout the country. Fish are plentiful along the coast and in Cameroon's rivers and lakes.

Courtesy of Dr. Walter Blue

The market in Bamenda offers a variety of seasonal produce and a vital means of socializing. Markets are usually held daily in urban areas and occur less frequently in rural regions.

This woman is making *boule* by gradually stirring *gari*—cassava flour—into boiling water. The sticky mixture is then dipped into heavily spiced sauces made from meat and vegetables.

Courtesy of Dr. Walter Blue

Four-fifths of Cameroon's work force is employed on farms. Men usually tend crops that will be sold at market, while women cultivate the plots that feed the family. In both instances, tools are simple, and livestock often provide muscle power.

4) The Economy

The Cameroonian economy represents one of few financial successes on the African continent. A combination of oil production and agricultural exports has kept Cameroon's economy growing at an impressive rate. The average yearly income for each Cameroonian was about $800 in the mid-1980s—a far higher figure than in many African nations. Great differences in income levels exist within Cameroon, however. Researchers in the 1980s found that 10 percent of the population receive 60 percent of the national income. The northern and eastern regions registered the lowest income levels, and the urbanized provinces along the coast and in the south had the highest.

Agriculture

Although the contribution of agriculture to the Cameroonian economy has declined since the 1970s, farming continued to employ 80 percent of the labor force in the late 1980s. Agricultural products provide about one-third of the nation's total export earnings, with coffee and cacao sales accounting for half of this amount. Cameroonian farmers—most of whom cultivate small plots of land—rather than large-scale, foreign landowners, supply almost all of the agricultural products for export. Rubber and palm oil, however, come from huge plantations that nonresident Europeans generally own.

The difficulties of Cameroon's agricultural economy are partly due to low and unpredictable world prices for the nation's exports. Also at fault is the wasteful management of some of the government-administered agricultural projects. Most farmers earn little income, in part because the government sets food prices at a low level.

Cacao bean pods—the source of chocolate—grow from the trunks of cacao trees. After harvesting, the beans inside the pods are allowed to ferment. Then they are dried to prevent mold from forming. Once they have been dried, the beans are ready for shipment or for further processing into candy.

Independent Picture Service

CROPS

Coffee production varies considerably from year to year but averages about 120,000 tons annually. Four-fifths of this coffee is a type called robusta, cultivated on the plains and plateaus of the south. The remaining one-fifth of the coffee crop is arabica, which is grown in the western highlands. Cacao beans, the source of chocolate, are planted mainly in the region around Yaoundé. Cacao output is around 110,000 tons annually, making Cameroon one of the world's largest suppliers. Coffee and cacao trees take many years to mature, and farmers have planted few replacement trees. As a result, Cameroon now faces the problem of trees that are aging, and therefore are less productive trees.

Cotton, introduced as a Cameroonian agricultural crop in 1950, is the main export of the northern region. Although hard hit by the droughts of the late 1970s and early 1980s, farmers have steadily improved cotton yields in recent years. Some farmers grow peanuts in the northern sandy soils, which are unsuitable for cotton. Part of the peanut harvest is exported, and the rest is processed into cooking oil.

The fruit of oil palms yields one of the most popular vegetable oils in the world. Processors extract the palm oil—one of Cameroon's main exports—from the pulp that surrounds the seeds.

Oil palm trees grow on plantations in the southern region. Although production has doubled since the late 1970s, the prices for Cameroon's palm oil do not compare successfully with Southeast Asia's. Cameroon's rubber exports, however, competed well on the world market in the late 1980s. Cameroonians cultivate rubber trees in both the southeastern and southwestern areas of the country. Banana and tea crops also contribute to the nation's export earnings.

Cameroon has consistently increased its production levels of rice, maize (corn), millet, and cassava, but the growth of food crops has not kept up with Cameroon's expanding population. The rise in the number of urban dwellers makes larger demands on farmers, most of whom still use traditional agricultural techniques.

TRADITIONAL FARMING

In most farming villages, women generally cultivate crops that will be consumed locally, while men grow crops that will be sold. Most farms are owned by families and are usually under 10 acres. Farmers clear brush to create fields and

An agricultural worker examines corn plants at a research station in western Cameroon. Agricultural development receives substantial governmental funding.

53

Cameroonian farming techniques involve the slash-and-burn method of land preparation *(left)*. Farmers cut up trees and other large plants, which, along with grasses, are burned to clear the land for plowing and planting *(below)*. This method immediately makes the fields more fertile. Within three or four years, however, crops use up the nutrients in the soil. As a result, the land must lie unplanted for many seasons to regain its nutrients.

then cultivate these plots for three or four years until the soil loses its nutrients. The land then lies fallow (unplanted) for up to 25 years to regain its fertility, and farmers make new clearings for their crops elsewhere. In the western region, rich volcanic soils shorten the fallow period to three years.

Traditional agricultural activities in the north include livestock raising and planting crops along riverbanks with the aid of animal-drawn plows and a limited amount of irrigation. In southern Cameroon, farmers grow cassavas, taros (starchy roots), plantains (a type of banana), maize, sweet potatoes, and sugarcane. They also raise smaller amounts of tomatoes, beans, squash, pimientos, and tobacco.

On most farms, several crops are planted in a single field—a practice called mixed cropping. This mixing of crops mimics the pattern of plant growth in the rain-forest. Several layers of crops grow at varying levels: above the ground, on the ground's surface, and underground. The variety of plants guards against the possibility of crop diseases or pests wiping out an entire field. Mixed cropping also raises plants that ripen at different times of the year, offering a steady food supply to the farmer's family.

Fishing and Forestry

Fishing is an important industry in Cameroon, and the total catch is estimated at

Courtesy of L. Everett

Cattle are raised mostly in northern Cameroon, where grazing land is plentiful. Many livestock are afflicted by nagana—a deadly disease transmitted by tsetse flies.

75,000 tons per year. Fishermen catch about 20,000 tons of freshwater fish in the nation's rivers and lakes, especially in Lake Chad. Because of boundary disputes with Nigeria over ocean territory, Cameroon's fishing area on the Gulf of Guinea is limited. Nevertheless, commercial fishing vessels, including shrimp boats, set out from Douala and bring in about 20,000 tons of saltwater fish per year. A large number of fishermen also work the ocean waters, taking in an estimated 35,000 tons per year.

Workers at a fish farm in Cameroon collect their nets from a grass-enclosed pond.

Courtesy of Agency for International Development

Courtesy of Dr. Walter Blue

Rural Cameroonians rely almost exclusively on wood for cooking fuel. Women often carry loads of firewood on their heads as they return to their villages.

Europeans began purchasing Cameroonian timber at the end of the nineteenth century, and potential exists for increased timber earnings in the twenty-first cen-

tury. Forests cover almost half of Cameroon, and nearly one-third of this area is being logged. Increased production depends on an improved road system, which will allow exporters to reach other countries. Despite efforts of the Cameroonian government to increase local participation, large foreign firms dominate the harvesting of teak, mahogany, and ebony.

Mining and Energy

In 1976, after several years of exploration, Elf (a French oil company) discovered oil in the Cameroonian waters of the Gulf of Guinea. Production started the next year, and an oil processing plant opened at Limbe. Explorers found new deposits off the coast near Nigeria in 1984. Oil output increased into the late 1980s, but the lack of continued exploration means an eventual loss of production once Cameroon's small sources of oil are depleted.

The Cameroonian government's oil revenue was about $4 billion from 1980 to 1985. Declining oil prices in the late 1980s

Courtesy of A. B. Hinderlie

Cameroon's coastal seafloor contains small supplies of oil. In the early 1980s, offshore drilling platforms extracted petroleum worth $4 billion.

The swift rivers that flow through many parts of Cameroon have the potential to produce a large amount of hydroelectricity, which already provides nearly all of the country's power.

The government offers tax breaks to encourage private enterprises, such as this large-scale agricultural estate on the Adamawa Plateau. Most privately owned farms have less than 10 acres of land.

Foreign investments have helped Cameroon improve its economy. This agricultural research station at Bambui tries to develop hardy, high-yielding strains of corn and other crops.

reduced Cameroon's oil income. Nevertheless, the nation received enough revenue from oil to make up for uncertain agricultural prices. Offshore natural gas fields have yet to be fully explored. Southern deposits of iron ore and northern reserves of bauxite (from which aluminum is made) are also untapped.

Hydroelectricity provides almost all of the country's power. The government constructed two major dams—one at Edéa and another one farther north—on the Sanaga River. The Lagado Dam, built on the Benue River with assistance from the People's Republic of China, began operating in 1986. An aluminum smelting plant at Edéa uses up more than half of the nation's energy supply.

Industry and Trade

Cameroon's manufacturing sector is small but has increased steadily since independence, with especially rapid growth in the 1980s. Cameroonian industry consists mainly of processing plants for local or imported raw materials and of assembly factories for imported components. About 200 small firms produce consumer goods such as plastics, beer, cigarettes, chocolate, and textiles. Cameroon imports large machinery and other manufactured goods.

The largest industry in the nation is ALUCAM, a jointly owned French and Cameroonian aluminum smelting complex located at Edéa. In the 1980s bauxite was imported from Guinea. This arrangement may change, however, when the bauxite deposits in northern Cameroon are mined and are efficiently linked to the coast by way of the Trans-Cameroonian Railway. ALUCAM's aluminum sales contribute significantly to Cameroon's economy.

The government encourages private initiative through tax incentives, giving new companies low tax rates. This policy has generally helped large-scale foreign enterprises that have money ready to invest, although small and medium-sized ventures are now being favored.

France is Cameroon's main trading partner. In the mid-1980s, France purchased 33 percent of Cameroon's exports and supplied 43 percent of the nation's imports. The Netherlands buys much of Cameroon's petroleum and is the country's second largest export buyer, followed by the United States, Italy, and Germany.

Cameroon exports more than it imports, which means it earns more money than

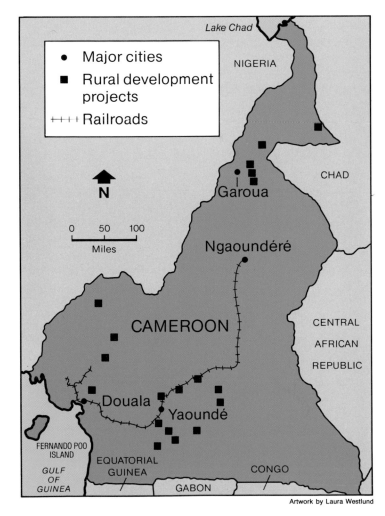

In the 1970s, the Cameroonian government's five-year economic plans concentrated on developing rural areas—including the expansion of towns and the building of roads and railways.

Artwork by Laura Westlund

59

it spends. Much of this surplus revenue goes to projects that are favored in Cameroon's five-year development plans. Formed by government economists, the development plans set growth targets for industry and agriculture and recommend how to invest government, private, and foreign funds.

Transportation

The size and quality of the transportation network in Cameroon compare favorably with the transportation systems in many neighboring African nations. Roads between the major cities are good, including the new Yaoundé-Douala road. Expansion, however, is necessary for continued economic growth. Less than five percent of Cameroon's 38,439 miles of roads are paved. Unpaved surfaces in the rainiest areas are often unusable for months at a time, and many villagers are unable to take their crops to market. Cars are rare in Cameroon, and only 1 out of every 120 Cameroonians owns an automobile.

In the 1970s and 1980s, the nation's railway system doubled to over 600 miles of track. Completed in the mid-1970s, the nation's biggest rail project is the Trans-Cameroonian Railway that links Ngaoundéré with the port of Douala. Another

The Trans-Cameroonian Railway—the nation's biggest rail project—connects Ngaoundéré and Douala. This rail link helped Cameroon's railway system double in size to over 600 miles of track.

A narrow trail guides patients in a rural area to a local clinic. Many regions of Cameroon are connected by footpaths.

Photo by Bernice K. Condit

important project has been the reconstruction of the Douala-Yaoundé rail line, which has substantially reduced travel time between the two cities.

Ninety-five percent of Cameroon's ocean traffic goes through Douala. The port continues to grow, and it can now handle seven million tons of goods a year. Kribi, a town on the southern coast, is also being developed to handle more timber and mineral shipments both for Cameroon and the Central African Republic.

Bamenda's residents contribute one day per week to building a bridge, which eventually will allow people of southwestern Cameroon to cross this river easily and safely.

Courtesy of United Nations

Photo by Daniel H. Condit

At the height of Cameroon's rainy season, roads are hazardous. Vehicles may slide off the unpaved thoroughfares, which can become seas of mud from April to October.

About 75 percent of Cameroon Airlines is nationally owned, and a French firm holds the remaining 25 percent of the company. The airline serves about a dozen cities in Africa and Europe. Cameroon's main international airport is located at Douala, with another major airfield at Garoua. Similar facilities were being built at Yaoundé in the late 1980s.

Future Challenges

President Biya introduced the nation's sixth five-year plan in July 1986. The plan strongly emphasizes agricultural development, with the rural sector slated to receive one-fourth of the government's investment resources during this five-year period. Transportation, manufacturing, housing, and social services are also given priority for development in the new plan.

As Cameroon's oil revenues fell to a new low in 1986, President Biya cut back national spending, in part by reducing housing benefits for government employees. For the first time since independence, the government's annual budget shrank, dropping from $2.7 billion in 1986 to $2.2 billion in 1987.

Political challenges to Biya's regime have resulted in reforms and in increased democratic participation. The government hopes to encourage more cooperation between English-speaking and French-speaking Cameroonians and to ease the tensions between northerners and southerners. Many Cameroonians have mixed reactions to the slow progress, especially in the area of political reform, made by the government.

Although Cameroon depends heavily on foreign financial aid and technology, the nation has achieved middle-income status among developing countries. Cameroon's diverse potential resources—including hydroelectric power, untapped bauxite deposits, and opportunities for agricultural expansion—form the basis for the nation's continued good prospects.

Rural areas were scheduled to receive one-fourth of the government's investment resources as part of the five-year plan introduced in 1986. Agricultural development is strongly supported as a means of improving the standard of living in Cameroon.

Courtesy of Dr. Walter Blue

Courtesy of American Lutheran Church

With an increase in government funds to improve services, these young Cameroonians may be able to enjoy a more comfortable style of life than their parents had and greater access to health care, education, and job opportunities.

Index